Snakeberry Mamas

Charlotte Lit Press
Charlotte Center for Literary Arts, Inc.

PO Box 18607
Charlotte, NC 28218

charlottelit.org/press

Cover image by Penta Springs Limited
Author photo by Chris Chavira, Lem Lynch Photography

ISBN: 978-1-960558-12-1

PROUD MEMBER

[clmp]

COMMUNITY OF LITERARY MAGAZINES & PRESSES
W W W . C L M P . O R G

Snakeberry Mamas

Words from the Wild

Mary Alice Dixon

for Mary Allred Crews & Julie Gaillard Suk
my first poetry teachers
women who gave me the courage to set words on fire

and

for James Steven Hinson
my beloved son
whose holy music gives me the inspiration to sing

Contents

Preface

I first encountered the poetry of place through my West Virginia grandmother. Granny, a blind seamstress, collected buttons she could not see, buttons kept in tins she said reminded her of mountain caves. Born Delilah Sharps in 1880, Granny was a hardscrabble artist who found landscapes with her hands. She came from old Quaker stock, a people imprisoned for their beliefs in 17th century England—a people who endured high seas and smallpox, sailing to what was called a New World. They lived, or so the story goes, in the boughs of a fallen tree.

Granny Delilah's old Quaker roots were overgrown with mountain magic and ornery defiance. She lived with my parents and me, planting her West Virginia ways in my head and heart.

My grandfather, born in 1875, also lived with us. A newspaper reporter given to tall-tale-telling, he claimed to have once won a bet by going over Niagara Falls in a wooden barrel. He survived the Falls, he said, with nary a scratch. He enjoyed the fittingly named chew-tobacco, "Bull of the Woods." From Grandpa I learned the magic of memoir spun into myth.

From my father, a scholarly steel worker who put himself through night school to become an engineer, I learned an architecture of faith. Daddy designed airplane parts in WWII and drafted blueprints of angel wings. He discovered the mechanics of how feathered wings could carry the Ark of the Covenant. He looked for the Holy Grail. I still have his drawings.

My mother was born in a cottage in West Virginia. She penned poems in her stenography notebooks while working as a secretary during the Great Depression. She wrote in a calligraphic shorthand. Her writings look like secret cave paintings. Mama taught me poetry can flourish in the margins. I still hear her voice.

The places and people appearing in *Snakeberry Mamas* comprise the autobiography of my family stories, my memories, and my dreams. Like Daddy's drawings of angel wings, the Appalachian landscapes I call Witcher, Witcher River, Hungry River, and Bald Butt Mountain are real places. You can also find them on United States Geological Survey maps of West Virginia and North Carolina.

Mary Alice Dixon
Charlotte, NC

"You were once wild here. Don't let them tame you."

Isadora Duncan

Snakeberry Mama

Mama wove spells in snakeberry garlands,
      wore them in her hair.
Witch eyes for the moon, she said,
      polka-dot fruit circling her head.

Taught me to howl when I bled,
      make the moon rise
in Appalachian skies,
      redden the Blue Ridge dusk.

Bred in Mama's root craft and thread,
      her charms sewn in my head,
I lived in lust for the moon.

Then Mama died.

Keening her loss, growling my grief,
      I womaned into wild.

Now on rare red nights
      when Blood Moon shines bright
when sky's Snake Stars align, I follow
      Mama's ways

leaving my bed to twine my fingers
      in snakeberry rings,
sowing circles, weaving spells

with my pink-petaled pollen-powdered
      sweet-poison-berry vines.

I shift my shape with chant, in dance,
      my mother in me in trance
til the hills holler Mama.

Howls wet my tongue.
      Snakeberries coil in my hair.
Moon bleeds my name.

Autobiography of a Smoky Mountain Magnolia

On blue banks
of the Hungry River
my branches
sheltering
maidenhair ferns
I hold blossoms
sprung from roots
born before the creation
of bees.

I open
the female part
of my flower
to pollen to petal to flower
so tough
beetle mandibles
cannot break me
or the buds
of my unborn daughters.

So tough
I seed myself alone
to survive
the unsurviving time
like a mountain
who does not need
honeybees to avalanche
her stone.

Granny Explains Rebirthing to Me

When you die
Granny tells me

the owl women
brush you
with wishbones and wings

rub you with tung oil
and yarrow-laced butter

tender your body
to tinder

til only the scent of yarrow
lingers, like ashes
in smoke.

Then you sail your soul
home, girl, home
on a birch bark boat, home

to Blue Ridge hollers
far across
Witcher River waters

where heart rings
of pine
survive the dying

like ghosts on a boat,
like the smell of yarrow
in wishbones and smoke.

Then I remember
the memories of mothers,
the sweet in the butter

circle of ashes,
cradle of heart rings

the birthing, the branching,
the light brush of wings.

Granny's Helpings

Only in the wake
of Granny's passing
did I hear

of the Starving Time,
the coal miners' strike in 1929
when Witcher Way Holler

survived
on the cast-off crumbs
of rich men's crusts
and shreds
of company script.

Whispers in the wake
of Granny's passing
told of her helpings of mercy

nursing the hollow
into the full,
feeding the hungry
into the earth

how poppets in bloodroots
taught Granny

the secret poison
of witchberry brew

the healings
of conjure spiced stew,
the curings
of red pickled eggs
with foxglove seeds,
of scuppernong wines
with angel trumpet leaves.

Only then did I learn
how bloodroot can hurt,
how grief
can make knife blades
of red pickled eggs

how Granny ended
the starving
by speeding the dying,
serving mercy
thick with hemlock
grown in dark Witcher dirt.

Granny was a Goosebone Prophet

who told the weather
in colors of bones, said
the dark in the marrow
tells the coming of cold.

But then winter weakened.
Earth warmed, seas rose
plastic and hot.

Granny's snake vines fruited
fiery berries. Her goosebones
grew pale. Her brown hair
turned white.

She braided her vines
into basket she wore as a hat,
then hid her goosebones
in a chest built with cedar,
christened with spit.

Granny said she would soon
nest her soul in the cedar
but first she saved
the last dirty chunks
of Witcher River ice,
dark cubes of cold
she called grounds of hope.

She placed one on my tongue,
saying I must muscle myself
to save autumn. Told me
spring is the lover of fall.
Then she was gone.

Winter is dead. The
cedar chest buried.
But Granny's hat still holds
memories—
ice edging the river,
goosebones shining
dark, the color of hope.

Prick of the Dark

With snakeberry hat
on my head,
I hold one holly leaf
to holy
Granny's grave
with goosebones,
eggshells, prickly
pinecones that cut
my palm.

Silly, I say to myself,
silly girl, you
with your old
mountain offerings
to the dead.
How, after all,
can grief be
a thing graspable?
Or holy be
a thing held?
Silly girl.

Then the point
of the holly pierces
my thumb.

I open my hand
bleeding, I stain the dirt
red, dark like the juice
of snakeberry fruit.

Granny Tells of Grace

When I was young, Granny told me,
Aunt Grace, the tailor woman,
taught me how to find the muscle
in my fingers

the backbone in my hands, how
to cut a belt to fit the flesh I wore,
not what others wished I was.

Some say old Grace is dead now,
Granny said, *buried with the seeds*
of wind-thrown apple trees under
Graveyard Fields.

But my eyes have seen Grace rise,
moon-fat and spirit-wise, spinning
stars, unfastening Orion's belt.

Look up. See the threads of Grace
sewing revolution.

She works with God the Mother,
expanding heaven's seams.

Wild Nutmeg Sparks Revolution

Even naked I wear my many bodies,
  remembering the garden
where my many arms grew many
   blossomed hands, branching free
on wild Witcher nutmeg tree, wet
  to flower in April-birthing shower.

But now in December's dying sun, I am
   summoned to your winter kitchen
with its papered grapevine walls
   in their quiet-seeming sleep
beside the Frigidaire, I am taken, hard
  to your cutting board

ground to slivers of spice, I wear a fragrant
   mask, seasoning that old family
recipe for mom's apple pie, fruit of the garden
   tree of the snake, snare of the witch
with sugared Red Delicious. But taste me alone
  hot with oven heat.

I will tear off your tongue with the bite
   my flowers never had, and grapevine
sister of my many arms, will spring to coil
   around your neck, she
with her many fruited hands, resistance
  awakened by my scent.

Britches with Balls & Yellow-Pleated Parasols: Suffragette's Recipe

Dick-devil claws in her jaws
        stinging nettles in her hair

Sister Cecil stands at the crossroads
        wearing boots with blue stockings

stirring women
        with hot sauce and spice, chanting

Cast off your corsets and lady-slippers,
        cast off your locks and your lockets.

Abandon your rue and your weeds.
        I give you my recipe

for a dish I call britches with balls, hot
        under yellow-pleated parasols.

First, scrape fear from your flesh.
        Lace bone to your back. Gather

your muscle and marrow. Add salt
        to your cider and sorrows.

Bring tears to a boil.

Season with rye, the slights of your kin
        the scars of your skin.

Add boots, leather britches, and wings.
        Stir, stir, stir. Add yeast. And teeth.

Then serve with the pricks
        of poison-pleated parasols.

Serve suffrage with pepper and helpings
        of tongue.

Speak up with the claws in your jaws
        and the points of your parasols.

Feed your daughters
        with ballots and wings.

Night Owl Dreams Woman

In sunrise sleep
between the silver lichen
and the straw,
you dream yourself
a woman

wearing muscles
on your legs,
feathers in your hair,
secrets
in your flesh.

At sunset
you wake again,
wings stretching
from your breast,
mysteries hatching
in your nest

as hungry cries
break from eggs,
a woman lies
in hope and silk
to dream she sleeps

with you,
warms her brood
with feathers, feeds
them with her milk.

I Spoke Feathers

As a child, I spoke feathers
and nested my limbs
beneath Granny's cedars,
becoming a bird,
speaking feathers
I pasted on paper
humming
a language of wings

lost—

until tonight
in April twilight
I hear birch bark echo
the cinnamon songs
of sharp-shinned hawks

out on a limb
feathers the color of rust.

I dip in song
and rise full-throated
woman-winged, wild.

Song of Goat Stew in the Village of Women

Time
tore a wound on the night
of the big-bellied moon,
cutting a valley
I followed
across the Bald Butt Mountains
to the village of women
at the edge of a blood red river.

Caught
in clouds of goat's rue,
circles of broom,
smell of goat,
heat of stew,
thistle of gristle,
witches' brew,
crunch of bones,
in the village of women
at the edge of a blood red river.

Spun
in the cookery-butchery
owl-winging dance
of crooning crones,
their blood-bleating chants
that led to the bed
of flesh-spiced brew

the night the moon
grew new
in the village of women
at the edge of a blood red river

Bite
of the sauce that wet
the mouth of the salty one
who took me to bed,
the tang of her hair, her head
her fox-tendon thread,
knotted and beaded
and dowry-rich red,
the ripening moon,
the wild wet river
flooding my womb
with the song
of the goat,
boiled alive, its cries
frothing the river
to white water falls.

How the Witcher Witch Celebrates
the Vernal Equinox

Let me tell you, Green Man,
how I wore winter
in my heartwood until this night,
at the end of onyx days

when Blue Ridge Mountain sage
silks the sky with song,
when mats of velvet moss
brocade my trunk with spring.

This holy day of goddess fire,
I paint my eggs with blood,
dancing light and lichen,
I seed your bed with flame.

Lifting up your limbs,
boughing down your branches,
I teach you how to pray.

When you kneel before me
I taste acorns in the wildfire
of your tongue.

Witcher Woman Feeds Hungry Man

In the Smoky Mountain steam
by the dirt yard cook fire,
back bent from kneading,
hands fat from flour,
strong stands
the woman,
unfallen, offering
her bread, unleavened,
salted with pepper and thorns,
bearing
the scent of saffron and sin.

Take and eat,
she says. Taste
the grains
of my Witcher Way wheat.

In the steam
by the dirt yard cook fire
Witcher woman,
hungry man,
coming together,
hard wheat and wine.

Praying in flesh,
divining
the shared peace of bread,
divining
the hot bite of God.

Woman Seizing Power

They call me Snakeberry Mama
married to the moon,
they call me Witcher Witch
      with my birch wood broom.

And I say Yes. Yes, I am
a fury lit with flame
a woman feared by sophists
      who dress in dying legal habits

who cannot tame me
to their holy orders or bridle me
to chaste domestication. So they seek
      to burn me at the stake.

But I wield the weight
of women wedded to their rights.
And I say
      Now. Now.

Come, my magic broom,
shift shape with me, be witch
with me, until only
      unquenched fires remain.

In this red hour we will sweep
the earth with others of our kind

rising up
      sisters in revolt.

And I say Yes. Yes,
we grow
nails like dragon scales,
      bones of crones, bitches

we witches, fierce-lived, battle-wise.

Snakeberry Mama's Communion with Orange

Blind after the burning,
I lie in cloak of dark,
deep under wet-petaled irises,
my body re-members
herself.

Remembers how you,
sweet orange,
once peeled yourself
for me like a lover
displaying your flesh

tang savored slowly
even now on the tip
of my tongue.

Though my eyes sleep
in night, morning orange
kisses my lips, her juice
chalices my chin.

Mouth open, eyes closed,
I love blindly, zest blessing
my mouth.

I become, wholly, the fruit
I see, barely by the skin
of my old soft teeth.

God the Woman Comes with Tongue of Fire

When barren pasture
pleads, come,
thou holy ghost,
heal the broken
hearts of trees

I turn from dove
to woman, torches
on my sleeves.

I find you, silver birch,
your flesh
encased in scar,
your limbs
storm broken raw.

I unpeel you
of your rough,
strip you
of your skin,
bind your wood to me.

You cry your name
is lost.
I tell you it is fire,
kindle you
to Pentecost,
baptism by desire.

Your bark
upon my breath,
your splinters
on my breast,
in cinders
of your blaze

I rebirth
the Easter earth,
seed your ashes
in her dirt
and green life
as I May.

It is done.

I rise again to dove,
your halo
burning on my tongue.

Blood Moon Sends Me Love Letters on Apple Skins

Letters I read with my tongue,
words from the wild
where talk is a touch
and touch is a god
I can taste.

Yes.
I answer
Yes to the fruit
of the tree.
Yes to the world my tongue
offers me.

Yes
to the knowing sea
where blood moon
marries me
to me

as hunger carries me
from eve to dawn
with opened eyes,
pregnant
with light, seeded
with sight,
sowing
the Red Delicious
of Yes.

Aunt Lil's Crazy Quilt

Aunt Lil packed a pistol
with her words,
said she once
nearly killed a man
talking him to death,
then she laughed, loud
as pistol shot.

Fearless
backwoods woman,
from Independence Mountain,
Lil died
the day a rattler bit her
at the Witcher
Hallelujah Tent Revival.

Preacher, sermonizing,
said the serpent's bite
was God's good kiss
sweet talkin' Aunt Lil
home.

Lil gone,
I slipped beneath her quilt,
a patchwork
made of burlap corn feed bags,
coarse-seamed
with gingham apron scraps.

Hiding there,
I heard Lil's gingham whisper,
thick as clover honey,
"Learn from me, girl,
no matter what
those preachers say,
it's not snakes
that gets a gal to heaven.
Try lust for starters,
honey child,
but you gotta finish up
with love."

Then I heard Lil's burlap laugh,
rough as red clay fields,
and through the years
I've learned
Lil's ragged quilt was right.

Wild Witcher River Rose Meets Tree Swallow

Buried in dirty March sleet,
spine bent
in Easter icing,
I branch bare at the edge
of white waters,
share roots with snakeberry vines
and Appalachian coal.

I pray you
understand,
bright-feathered bird,
I'm not looking for you
in the hungry needs
of comfrey root weaves,
or in the hard hurt
seeds of Job's Tears
buried in corn beads.

No, I'm not looking
for you at all.

But from the skies
halleluiah surprise.

When you nest
in my thickets
there is no winter.

Tangled together
we dream the melting.

Your iridescent wings
bring me to spring;
when you sing
I am rose.

In a Hungry River Compost Pile

After the storm,
grounds of dark

fall, coffee grounds
seeping

through bark and buried
birch leaves,
through cardamom curls
of old orange skins,
wilted iceberg lettuce,
crushed comfrey
with fenders
and

the shell of my house,
a pottery wheel,
the promise to hold,
like a cup, broken.

Hungry,
the Appalachian river,
hungry, the grit
in the grounds

seeking
resurrection of dirt
from water

seeping, still

in the cinnamon-red roots
of madder and bloodwort,
planted in mud,
the grounds of my life

seeking
resurrection from water

seeking earth
worm-fat, wet and dirty.

Compost Your Heart to Green

Spring woman, Snakeberry Mama,
rise

from Granny's bloodroots,
and Witcher River mud.

April your body
in red azalea dreams.

Sew yourself wild
in silver-skinned onions.

Feed yourself wise
with sassafras and sage.

Sing light, Mama,
in the mother tongue of rain

as pine bark falls
in open love with you.

Grow old
in ghosts of chestnut shade

as Smoky Mountains peak
with bald triumphant age.

And you are ready
not to die.

Compost your heart to green.

Spring woman, Snakeberry Mama,
rise

again

from roots resisting all
that does not birth from dirt.

October Hands

Mama, tough Carolina cracker,
hands muscled flesh
under lilac lacquer;
hands that made her "hard work
happiness cakes,"
thick knuckled with nuts,
kneaded with thumbs,
old purpled plums;

hands that waved
when she answered
the call of hailing sky,
danced
down Providence Road,
to fly
where the path
narrows to nothing,
where the shoulder
ambushes the foot,
where she fell.

I see Mama's October hands
in me,
tulip blood in winter skin,
fingers laced
to her ladder-back chair,
then folded

in prayer,
hands holding the shape
of the woman
who carried them there,
tough Carolina cracker,
muscled flesh
under lilac lacquer.

Falling in Love at Appalachian Gems, Geodes & Bark Art Café

At the end of Witcher Way
  where the wild rose meets
the bittersweet and the witchgrass
  roots in clay, I wander

through a roadside café, look
  through an open window
and fall in love
  with the landscape of you

stretched on a blue ridged canvas
  your face brushed with feathers
of finch, flesh etched with clear cuts
  of blade, footprints of crow.

Oil slicks wet your lips, smoke clouds
  weigh your brow. I see
your sorrows in veins stained with lead,
  the hurt of your dirt for green.

With you in my eyes, I paint roses
  with witchgrass
and bittersweet leaves, drawing you,
  on my knees

calling calling calling
  your name

as if

        there is no other
        mother

my earth my god
my first and last lover.

Glossary of Plants, Creatures, & Folklore Customs

Acorn: seed of oak tree; child of the immortals who dwell in oaks, acts as a bridge between the sensual and the spiritual worlds

Angel Trumpet: highly toxic small tree with pendulous trumpet-shaped flowers; ingestion brings death to mortals lured by its intoxicatingly sweet fragrance; facilitates communication with the ghosts

Apple: edible fruit widely cultivated since ancient times; in some mountain traditions considered both the food of lovers and the food of the gods, associations derived from the biblical Song of Solomon in which the beloved calls "the lover" an apple tree; the Eden "tree of the knowledge of good and evil" is also often said to be an apple tree

Azalea: flowering shrub, most varieties are evergreen; repels both wickedness and winter; bestows dreams of healing transformation

Balls: a.k.a. *Fireball Tomatoes*, a variety of tomato, an edible vegetable in the nightshade family with a tart taste, meaty flesh, glossy red skin; fireballs may be used in cleansing rituals as their scarlet color suggests blood baths and birthing

Birch: fast-growing deciduous hardwood tree with thin bark that peels off in paper-like layers; called the most feminine of trees; birch is the first letter of Ogham, the ancient Celtic tree alphabet; the wood of choice for the brooms of Appalachian seers and witches; she who wields a birch broom drives out evil, awakens sensual love, engenders fertility

Bittersweet: toxic plant in the nightshade family; its fine-toothed, glossy leaves symbolize duality, warding off malevolent forces, and protecting benevolent spirits

Bloodroot: woodland perennial in the poppy family having large-lobed leaves, orange-red sap, highly toxic roots; it spreads through multiple generations in colonies some call invasive; the smoke of burning bloodroot cleanses those who have seen apparitions of the dead

Britches, a.k.a. *Leather Britches:* green string beans, make a snapping sound when their pods are broken; when preserved by being hung to dry like pants on a clothesline the beans harden, thus giving rise to the name *leather britches* or, simply, *britches*

Butter: dairy product made from churned cow or goat milk; if rubbed into skin, it is believed to regenerate the body; also the name *butter* is applied in some mountain traditions to a yellow jelly-like fungus at the base of very old trees; the fungus is also known as *fairy butter* and is given as offerings to the spirits of the dead

Cardamom: a herbaceous perennial whose seeds make an aromatic spice; used in cooking, body painting, and aphrodisiac love potions; when dried to a pale yellow cardamom pods are employed in rituals of regeneration

Cedar: coniferous tree with winged seeds and rot-resistant wood; considered the tree of longevity and endurance, frequently cited in the Old Testament as a symbol of resilience; cedar's aromatic wood repels invasive insects, attracts ancestral spirits, and invites good spirits to nest in its rings

Chestnut: large deciduous tree whose wood was used for Appalachian cabins, coffins, and canoes; in the twentieth century a devastating blight wiped out most North America chestnut forests though a few ancestor trees survived; the chestnut tree is said to link the worlds of the living and the dead

Cinnamon: rust-red spice made from inner peels of tree bark; used in culinary preparations as well as in spirit cleansing rituals; cinnamon accelerates magic spells; cinnamon brooms sweep away suffering; legends tell of a giant cinnamon bird whose wings span the horizon when it sings

Comfrey, a.k.a. *Knitbone,* a.k.a. *Bruisewort:* an invasive flowering perennial herb used in folk medicine topically to treat broken bones and bruised skin; illegal to eat because toxic if ingested; comfrey roots are thick, tangled, and used to magically sew the torn to healing whole

Corn: tall cereal plant whose kernels are not only eaten but also used in divination and as prayer beads because of corn's regenerative nature

Dick-Devil Claws: perennial shrub-like herb whose seed pods resemble claws; its sharp-spiked fruit repels evil spirits; the addition of the word "dick" refers to a part of the male anatomy; the tuberous roots of *Devil Claws*, sometimes used to alleviate pain, can be poisonous

Egg: small hard-shell containing an embryo and laid by a female chicken or reptile; used in ritual cleansing, the egg absorbs evil; when painted red, egg shells signify and invoke fertility; to repel evil a person's name and a good intention are written in red on an egg shell, then the shell is bound in yard and buried, as if seeding the earth with hope

Finch: small bird with bright feathers; carries the souls of buried bodies; because of the bird's red markings it is known as the flame of the forest; feathers bound to twigs can be used as paint brushes

Foxglove, a.k.a. *Digitalis, Dead Man's Bells, Dead Man's Balls,* and *Witches' Gloves:* highly toxic flowering biennial; if the plant's flower is bent, a spirit is hiding inside; ingestion is fatal

Goat's Rue: herbaceous plant, its legumes, though mildly toxic, are sometimes given to mountain goats and women to increase mammary milk production; the plant's long tangled roots are called *Devil's Shoestrings;* its flowers are said to have pink wings

Goosebone Prophet: bones of dead geese are used by diviners to foretell the weather; dark blue streaks in the goose breastbones tell the diviner that the goose ate oily substances, like sunflowers seeds; the oil in the diet would help insulate the goose from frigid weather

Green Man: the mythic wild man of the woods; his body is part oak leaf and branch, an agile man with animal antlers and epic appetites

Happiness Cake: recipe includes 1 cup good thoughts, 1 cup kind deeds, 1 cup consideration, 2 cups sacrifice, 2 cups well-beaten faults, 3 cups forgiveness; this is from an old traditional recipe written on an index card by Mrs. Elvira Friend, a fourth-grade teacher in Charlotte, NC in the 1960s

Hemlock: toxic flowering plant, ingestion causes death; its flat oval seeds taste of lemon and parsley; said to carry the callings of lonely ghosts who want human companions in the afterworld

Iceberg Lettuce: pale crunchy leafy green vegetable; the name *Iceberg* arose in the 1920s when West Coast lettuce was transported by rail across North America in trains loaded with bins of ice; said by some to support rejuvenation

Lichen: vibrant hybrid growth of algae intertwined with fungus; lives on bare rock and on tree trunks; signifies resilience and partnership; used as nesting material, as dye for clothing; infused in oil or boiled in water, then used as tincture to enhance health and clairvoyance

Job's Tears: grain-producing perennial grass in warm climates, an annual in regions where frost occurs; its hard-shelled seeds often used for prayer beads

Lady Slippers: fragile orchids with delicate pink or white flowers; mature very slowly, can take up to sixteen years to grow from seed; in some mountain traditions the flowers are associated with innocent young girls who acquiesce to the commands of men

Madder: flowering perennial whose dark amber roots make a red dye; the hook-like hairs on its leaves and stems make madder a sign of pluck and persistence

Magnolia: ancient tree species, co-existed with dinosaurs, pre-dates bees; produces fragrant star-shaped flowers that may close at night; the female parts of the flowers, called carpels, are extremely tough

Maidenhair Fern: shade-loving green plant with feathery fronds; associated with secret feminine power and purity; in some Appalachian traditions the flickering of the fronds in the presence of a woman reveals that she is gifted in techniques of carnal knowledge

Moss: a non-flowering plant that thrives in damp areas; absorbs nutrients from air, rain, and dew; hanging moss is used as thread and can be woven into cloth; moss tucked inside a poppet becomes the poppet's heart; moss gathered from a gravestone brings goodness and is a reminder of the importance of prayer

Onion: pungent nutritious vegetable; slices of onion bulbs placed on the soles of the feet extract illness and impart rejuvenation; in witchcraft onion skin is used as a protective charm

Orange: juicy citrus fruit symbolizing fertility, passion, and creativity; orange peels hold memories of skin and identities shed, lost, and loved

Owl Women: mythic wise women of Appalachian legend; adept at shapeshifting from human to bird and back again; as owls can see in the dark, so owl women can see into the future

Nutmeg: popular spice made from an evergreen, used in culinary and medicinal practices; in granny magic nutmeg elicits erotic attraction, wards off evil demons, and amplifies spells

Pine: evergreen tree, symbol of immortality, despite cold winters and harsh lands, the pine endures, surviving, maintaining its green, regenerating its needles

Plum: sweet, juicy fruit; when dried, plum is called *Prune;* a *Plum Granny* is a fragrant, highly wrinkled variety

Poppet: enchanted doll made by hand from braided cornhusks, often stuffed with moss; houses ancestor spirits, giving them a place from which to cast spells in the world of the living

Rue: perennial herb with tiny yellow flowers and turquoise leaves; associated with regret, penance, and virginity; toxic if eaten in large amounts

Saffron: golden-orange spice made from crocus flower; the warmth of its color symbolizes divine light, especially the auras sometimes called halos

Sage: savory, aromatic herb with silver-gray leaves; where sage flourishes a woman dominates the land

Sassafras: fragrant deciduous tree; its bark wards off evil spirits; its wood is carved into charms that empower boys into virile manhood; toxic if ingested, though its leaves and flowers were once widely used in teas

Sharp-shinned Hawk: bird with large eyes, slender legs, long tail; bird of intuition; messenger between worlds

Snakeberries, a.k.a. *Poisonberry:* toxic fruit frequently mistaken for wild strawberries; tradition says the red berries are licked by snakes whose saliva deposits venom in the fruit; plants of enchantment, female magic, and protection against "the evil eye"

Stinging Nettle: flowering perennial herb; can grow up to nine feet; its sharp-toothed leaves are covered with hundreds of hollow needle-like hairs, each finer and sharper than a thorn; the sting of the nettle causes an intense burning pain

Tree Swallow: small songbird with iridescent teal back feathers; harbinger of spring, rebirth, and sensual love; carries messages between worlds and among plants, animals, and humans

Tulip: perennial flowering bulb in the lily family; blooms early in spring, signaling rebirth; spirits nest in its petals

Tung Oil: lubricant made from pressed seeds of tung trees, traditionally used as a varnish to waterproof wood, especially coffins and the hulls of wooden boats, occasionally used in folk embalming of corpses

Wild Rose: non-hybridized flower with five-petaled pink blossoms and large hips, the latter of which is used to make tea; symbolizes vitality and resilience; said to grow abundantly along the Cherokee Trail of Tears

Witchberry: common old-fashioned name for the toxic perennial also known as *Deadly Nightshade* and as *Belladonna;* these dark sweet berries are toxic, induce altered consciousness and death; witches derive magic flying powers from eating witchberries that kill mere mortals

Yarrow, a.k.a. *Death Flower* and *Devil's Nettle:* flowering perennial in the daisy family with fern-like leaves and tiny bright flowers; considered a feminine flower that protects the wearer, bolsters courage, imparts psychic powers; the smoke of burning yarrow elicits visions; when laid over eyelids yarrow imparts "second sight," including the ability to see into the future and into other worlds; yarrow stems, hung over doorways and cradles, offer the protection of a holy mother

Yellow-pleated parasol: poisonous yellow oval-capped mushroom; in folk tradition this mushroom foretells the death of a nearby plant; associated with feminine warrior spirits

Acknowledgements

Much gratitude to the editors of the following publications in which these poems, or earlier versions, sometimes with different titles, first appeared:

Appalachian Places: Stories from the Highlands (East Tennessee State University), "Granny Tells of Grace"

Bark & Blossom: "Compost Your Heart to Green"

Cathexis Northwest Press: "In a Hungry River Compost Pile"

Fourth River: "October Hands"

Gyroscope Review and *Gyroscope Review Year-End Anthology:* "Woman Seizing Power" (Nominated for Pushcart Prize in Poetry)

Gyroscope Review: "God the Woman Comes with Tongue of Fire"

Kakalak: "Snakeberry Mama," "Granny's Helpings," and "Aunt Lil's Crazy Quilt"

Main Street Rag: "Wild Nutmeg Sparks Revolution"

Moonstone Arts Center S/He Speaks: Voices of Women and Trans Folx: "Britches with Balls & Yellow-Pleated Parasols: Suffragette's Recipe"

North Carolina Poetry Society Poetry in Plain Sight Poster: "I Spoke Feathers"

Please See Me: "Snakeberry Mama's Communion with Orange" (North Carolina Poetry Society Poet Laureate Award Finalist)

Skeleton Flowers: "Granny was a Goosebone Prophet"

storySouth: "Prick of the Dark" (Winner, North Carolina Writers' Network Randall Jarrell Poetry Contest)

Sunlight Press: "Night Owl Dreams Woman"

The Yearbook of the Poetry Society of South Carolina 2025: "Witcher Woman Feeds Hungry Man" (Winner, John Edward Johns Prize)

Heartfelt gratitude to the brilliant poet and keen-eyed editor Kathie Collins, whose lyrical vision inspired, informed, and grew my work in more ways than I can ever count. Kathie gave generously of her time, abundant talent, and wisdom. I am grateful, too, to Paul Reali, technology genius and dazzling story writer. Thanks to Kathie, Paul, and to Paula Martinac for making Charlotte Lit a thriving creative community.

Deepest thanks to the women of my Charlotte Lit Chapbook Lab Cohort. You helped me paint in poetry the places I see in dreams: Helen Fowler, Morrow Dowdle, Jennifer Parker, Alida Woods, Caroline Wilson, Shannon Norwood, Libby Jenkins, Beth Shamaiengar, and Bobbi Campbell. Special thanks to my mentor, Stuart Dischell, who gave my work his time, attention, and razor-sharp wisdom. And to my other amazing mentors, Nickole Brown, AE Hines, and Lola Haskins, three superb and generous poets. The late Dannye Romine Powell offered me extraordinary support, without which this chapbook would not be.

This collection has also been shaped by the legendary Park Road Poets, under the great and graceful leadership of Peter Krones, a group that includes Paul Bruchon, Terence Cawley, Cheri Cox, Yael Grazier-Zerbarini, Carolina Kane Kenna, Sally Miller, John Oakes, Tom Weathers, and Randy White. Hats off, also, to my special circle of Café Poets: Bruce Bailey, John Clark, Chris Davis, Jerry Shinn, Lucinda Trew, and Helen Fowler. You make gladness happen.

Thank you, too, to the gifted Novant Health Hospice Team, for whom I help facilitate writing workshops: especially Sheri Lowe, Ivy Nguyen, Dena Evans, Kim Darden, Anna Kantsoios, Whitney Anders Bland, Nikola Taylor, Holly Warren, Ken Mitten, Cassandra Staley and all the bereaved who teach me about journeys of hope.

Bouquets to Sandy Hill, Nancy Zupanec, Patricia Joslin, and Linda Vigen Phillips, as well as to the great and infamous *Kiss My Ass Poet Babes*: Chris Avridson, Caroline Kane Kenna, and Sharon Kugelmas. And special thanks to my forever friends, *The Sunflower Sisters*: poets Mary Crews, Annette Gill, Sandra Logan, and Mishelle Mills. Our sisterhood is magic. Finally, endless gratitude for my family, especially my dear partner, Richard Ringley, and my beloved brilliant son, James Steven Hinson, without whom I would not be me. We share laughter, tears, and forever love.

About the Author

Born in Appalachian coal dust and reared in Carolina red clay, Mary Alice Dixon is an award winning poet, a gardener, and a teacher. She majored in Art History at Vassar College and did graduate work at Yale University. Her passion for gardening and history shaped her work as a professor of architectural and landscape history, which she taught at universities in Charlotte, Minneapolis, and China. She gave invited lectures on design history to audiences in Finland, Canada, and throughout the United States. She has also served as a Guardian ad Litem for abused children and an advocate for unhoused families. Mary Alice has long volunteered with hospice, reading poetry to the dying and facilitating writing workshops for the bereaved. She is a multiple Pushcart nominee, winner of both the North Carolina Writers' Network Randall Jarrell Poetry Competition and the Poetry Society of South Carolina John Edward Johnson Prize. Mary Alice is also a past finalist for the Broad River Review Rash Award in Poetry, the NC Writers' Network Doris Betts Fiction Prize and for the NC Poetry Society Poet Laureate Award. Her work is in scores of publications, including *Appalachian Places, Broad River Review, Fourth River, Gyroscope Review, Kakalak, Litmosphere, Main Street Rag, moonShine Review, Mythic Circle, Pinesong, North Dakota Quarterly, Stonecoast Review, storySouth*, and elsewhere. She lives in Charlotte where she talks to the ghosts of her dead cats, Thomas Merton and Alice B. Toklas, and grows sunflowers in cow manure. Find her at maryalicedixon.com.